I Know My Animals in English and Spanish

Aprender mis animales en inglés y español

by **Diego Maldonado**

Copyright © 2020 Diego Maldonado

ISBN: 9798619131064

PHOTOGRAPHY CREDITS

Andre Mouton

Hu Chen

Jonathan Cosens

Pinho

David Clode

Ansgar Sheffold

Harm Weustink

Henrique Setim

Allunix

Anshu

Mark Basarab

Dusan Smetana

I am an elephant. They call me Ellie.

Soy un elefante. Me llaman Ellie.

I am a monkey. They call me Mikey.

Soy un mono. Me llaman Mikey.

I am a bear. They call me Brandon.

Soy un oso. Me llaman Brandon.

I am a cat. They call me Coco.

Soy un gato. Me llaman Coco.

I am a cow. They call me Carol.

Soy una vaca. Me llaman Carol.

I am a dog. They call me Della.

Soy un perro. Me llaman Della.

I am a donkey. They call me Danny.

Soy un burro. Me llaman Danny.

I am a giraffe. They call me Gilbert.

Soy una jirafa. Me llaman Gilbert.

I am a koala. They call me KiKi.

Soy un koala. Me llaman KiKi.

I am an owl. They call me Oscar.

Soy un búho. Me llaman Oscar.

I am a penguin. They call me Petey.

Soy un pingüino. Me llaman Petey.

What am I?
ENGLISH
SPANISH

What am I?
ENGLISH
SPANISH

What am I?
ENGLISH
SPANISH

What am I?

ENGLISH

SPANISH

What am I?
ENGLISH
SPANISH

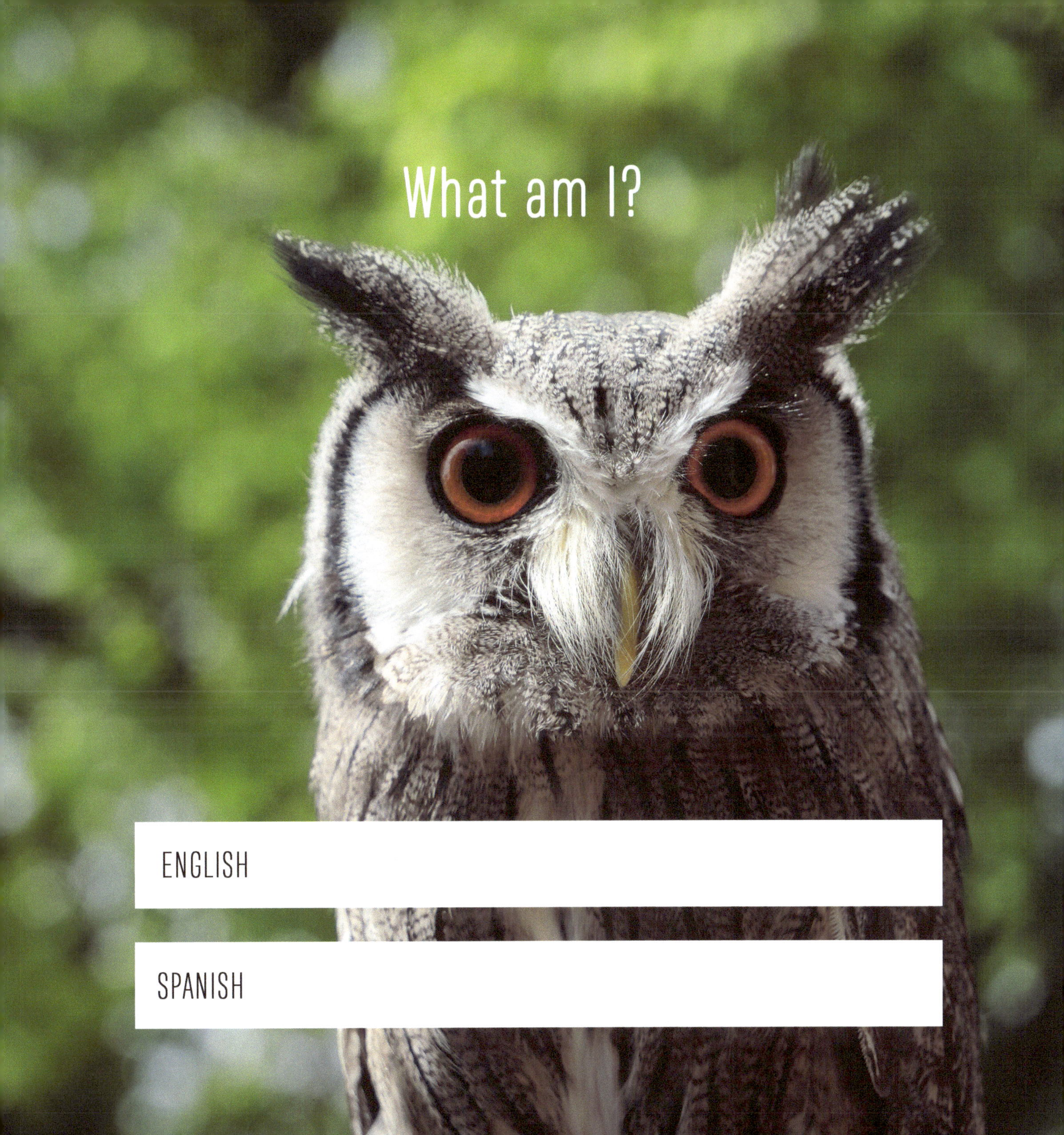

What am I?
ENGLISH
SPANISH

What am I?

ENGLISH

SPANISH

What am I?
ENGLISH
SPANISH

What am I?

ENGLISH

SPANISH

What am I?
ENGLISH
SPANISH

Can you flip through the book
and find an

OSO

Can you flip through the book
and find a

MONKEY

Can you flip through the book
and find a

JIRAFA

Puedes buscar una

COW

Puedes buscar un

PENGUIN

Can you flip through the book
and find a

BÚHO